Walking ᴛʜᴇ Burn

Rachel Kellum

Walking the Burn
©Rachel Kellum 2025

No part of this book may be reproduced by any means known at this time or derived henceforth without written permission of the publisher or author. The exception would be in the case of brief quotations embodied in the critical articles or reviews and pages where permission is specifically granted by the publisher or author.

Books may be purchased in quantity and/or special sales by contacting the publisher. All inquiries related to such matters should be addressed to:

Middle Creek Publishing & Audio
9161 Pueblo Mountain Park Road
Beulah, CO 81023
editor@middlecreekpublishing.com
(719) 369-9050

First Paperback Edition, 2025
ISBN: 978-1-957483-32-0
Cover Image: Rachel Kellum
Cover Design: Rachel Kellum

Walking the Burn

Rachel Kellum

Middle Creek Publishing & Audio
Beulah, CO   USA

Praise For *Walking The Burn*

The voice that inhabits the poems in this book is fearless and compassionate and in love with this life. Love of place, love of all sentient beings, love of family—*Walking the Burn* tells it all and tells it real, which must include the inevitable suffering we inherit as humans. As Rachel Kellum shows us in these poems, welcoming and fully engaging experience, all of it, can open us into the freedom of letting it go. In a time when so much of our bandwidth is bombarded with blah-blah and other static, I am grateful for her voice. Open this book and tune it in.

—**Peter Anderson**, author of *Riding the Wheel, Heading Home: Field Notes,* and *Reading Colorado: A Literary Road Guide* (recipient of the Colorado Book Award)

Among the many powerful qualities of Rachel Kellum's poetry is the sense it cultivates of life as a kind of respiration: breath in, breath out, breath held, breath released, and—in the end—breath returned to the air from which it was borrowed in the beginning. This is, in other words, poetry that arises from lived experience: family, friendship, love, loss, the passionate life of the mind and the mindful life of the passions. And for all that her readers will surely be grateful.

—**Joseph Hutchison**, Colorado Poet Laureate 2014-2019, author of *The World As Is: New & Selected Poems*

At the center of these brave and beautiful poems - like at the center of all things courageous - shines the grace, pain and responsibility of motherhood which blooms again and again. The arc of the poems and all that shines beneath is filled with tenderness in the midst of grief, betrayal, guilt and anger, yet Kellum reminds us, again and again, that love's flame is eternal, inexhaustible, dear and necessary. These poems sing with integrity, intelligence and intensity - so honest ... so very human ... so clear in their purpose - to heal all that are lucky enough to read their wisdom.

—**aaron a. abeyta,** recipient of The American Book Award, author of *Colcha* and *Rise, Do Not Be Afraid*

Walking the Burn sets ablaze the testament of family and motherhood. It unfolds a compelling narrative that demands to be heard and deeply felt, serving as a poignant reminder of our shared humanity. These poems reach out to embrace, to push away, to feel, to love. They celebrate love in all its forms—intense, tender, and unfiltered. Ultimately, these poems are a heartfelt exploration of love, presented in a most authentic and unyielding essence. Let your dog up on the couch, open this collection, and travel to where the fire stops burning. You'll find yourself in Rachel.

—**Julie Cummings,** Author of *Ride of My Life*, president of Columbine Poets, Inc., president of the National Federation of State Poetry Societies 2018-2022

Rachel Kellum fearlessly writes of all it means to be human in our present time. There is no denial or dismissal here. In *Walking the Burn* we are invited to share in a rich harvest of clear-eyed love and a litany of challenges met head on. We are shown the power and archetype of The Mother, the tenderness of The Lover, the sorrow of The Witness, the prescience of The Alchemist disguised as teacher. Kellum suggests "my stories will move and move through edgeless space like radio waves ..." She is right. Suffused with truth, visceral beauty, and resilience, her poems will endure in timelessness.

—**Barbara Ford,** author of *In Pursuit of Happenstance*, host of Poets and Minstrels on KHEN radio 2006-2025

For our courageous children

Foreword

If this collection had a color, it would be the vibrant green of the understory a year after a forest has burned. Have you seen it with your own eyes, too? How the places that were utterly consumed by wildfire become impossibly more verdant, more lush, more alive than the landscape nearby that was left untouched? *That's* the color.

It's a collection that could only be written by one who has burned—burned in the fires of childhood trauma. Burned in the early death of a younger sister. Burned in the suicide attempts of two sons. Burned through failed marriages. Burned by the failures of a nation to foster respect for all citizens. Burned by mental illness and self-blame.

And yet through all this burning, Rachel Kellum also shares with us what cannot be burned: Love.

My god. These are *love* poems. The hardest love poems. They speak of a human who turns toward what hurts the most and chooses love in the face of great ache. They speak of how a human might flourish not *in spite of* devastation, but *because of* devastation.

If the life lived is the burn, then these poems are paths through this charred landscape that allow us to not only see what is scarred and wounded, but also the astonishing beauty of how things—and people—heal.

At one time, the title of this book was *Inheritance*, and I loved that title for this collection, too, because poem after poem we see how intricately connected our lives are to all the choices and actions and circumstances of our ancestors. This book touches on six generations, and Rachel, in the middle, tugs on the threads that weave through them all. This is not only a telling of stories, it's also a letting go of them, a dissolving into love.

I admire this book for Rachel's skill as a poet—her layering of imagery, the playfulness with language and form. I admire the powerful arcs in the poems and the energetic thrust of the book as a whole. But most of all, I admire Rachel's vulnerability. When one person meets trauma and struggle with presence, it invites the rest of us to wonder if and how we can do that, too.

This is a book of healing. A humble book. A humbling book. A book with dignity. Integrity. A book that dares us, too, to walk through the burn of our lives toward forgiveness, mindful action, and love.

Rosemerry Wahtola Trommer
Placerville, CO
September 11, 2024

Contents

Arise

1

April 1971	19
Deep End	20
Quincy Grass	21
Little Rachel Dreams of Regeneration	23
The Story Goes	24
A Drift of Pigs	26
The Old Phones	28
I Can Never be 16 Again and Wouldn't Want to	29
My Sister's Arm	30
To My Little Sister, Dying	32

2

The Shell	37
Because my Son Announces *Narnia Trees!* on his Seventh Winter Solstice	38
Kate Chopin's Women	39
An Eight-Year-Old Boy	40
Walk	41
Picking Up Sons in a Parking Lot	42
Nests	43
After the Roast, Advice to an Angry Son	44
Bridge	45
And We Will Bloom	46
Who am I Now that I have Forgiven You	47
The Worst	48
How Often Do You Check on a Sleeping Baby?	49
Moving Home	50
The Mississippi of Motherhood	51
Walking the Green Belt	52
This His First Night Drive	53

3

Calculating a New Vocabulary of Joy	57
Tiny Birds	58
This is Not a Test	59
The Carpenter	60

Anatomy of a Mason Jar	62
American Gothic Koan	63
On Chickens: A Pastiche	64
Shed Dreams	66
A Year After the Abortion	67
Free Range Bunny Meets Brer Hare	68
Walking the Pasture	70
Building	71
Outside the Path of Totality	72
The Closest Ones the Brightest	74

Abide

Rufous-Sided Towhee	77
What We Could Not Let Go of	78
Sempervivum	79
One Friday Morning	80
Milky Way	81
Undraped	82
The Guitar	83
D-Con	84
Late Blooming	85
My Mother's Geraniums	86
False Metaphor	87
Feeding My Father	88
Icon	89
Final Grief	90
Faint Station	91
Vigil	92
Reteach a Thing its Loveliness	93
On Reading Woolf Again after 26 Years	94
To Measure Him	95
Shedding	96
Sage's Puja	97
Half Mud Half Slush	98
16 and 19	99
Ballistics	100
Minefields	101
Slow Touch	102
Your River	103
Retreat	104
Family Organism	105
List of Dreams for Yeshe Walmo	106
Fish Heads	107

Dissolve

Walking the Burn	111
Mountain Monsoon	112
Pietà	113
Keen	114
You Can Fill a Jar to the Top Twice	115
Blue Daughters	117
47	119
The Night before I turned 51	120
Hagstone	121
The Last Cut in Our Limited Series	122
Kids and Dogs	123
Rebeccanrachel	124
Holding On	125
Crossing Tacoma Bridges with My Pregnant Daughter	126
Sand Burial	127
Eclipse '24 for Grey, 24	128
Confluence	129
Four Days Past Due	130
Mother Dharma	131
Dissolving the Body	132
Notes	135
Acknowledgements	137
Special Thanks	138
About the Author	139
About the Press	141

Arise

1

April 1971

I found my ears' place
upright beneath her heart,
listening, a human
question mark resisting
some man's hands
pressing me through
muscle wall to write me
head down. Overnight
I righted myself against
my mother's music. He
pushed me down again
toward my birth,
but for my head.
Too large to pass,
he said, unlearned,
to Mother on her back.
He cut me out, red child,
her blood in my mouth,
lifted me into a world
where he made himself
hero and I made him
thief of my origin story.

Deep End

slick and sharp
as a new needle, as a girl
I forced myself

to jump feet first
incremental courage
nine feet, sixteen, thirty-three

pinching my nose
eyes clenched closed
belly coiling velocity

life rushed up stories
to swallow my inches
how we must live

stitching sky and water
to earth, back up for air
stitching us all together

we who don't belong
to each other, miles
of unknotted thread

trailing behind every dive
releasing the seam years
and years behind me

Quincy Grass

One eternal morning of childhood, the sun begins
to sift haze above the Mississippi River

before trees grab the lowering light. Not far away,
in a small subdivision full of muddy lots waiting

for houses and supplying children with the dirt clod
that will, tomorrow, bust open one boy's eyelid, a little girl,

the youngest of three children –the fragile, coddled one—
hunches in her pilled pink polyester nightgown over a small

fur-lined nest of baby rabbits at the bottom of the hill
behind her home. They look like the bottoms of her father's

Sunday naptime toes, nestled tight: absurd toes
with closed eyes, greasy transparent ears, tiny feet.

She gently strokes the back of each one. It is quiet.
Suddenly she is afraid. There is a stand of trees

behind her, shading where she squats in wet grass,
and beyond that, a long brick house holding her mother

vacuuming, or wiping from the kitchen table the dab
of milk beneath her cereal spoon, or looking out

the kitchen window above the sink, wondering where
Rachel has run off to. There she is. The girl pads barefoot,

panting openmouthed up the hill, through the sliding glass
door of the walkout basement, up carpeted stairs

into the dining room. "Mommy! There are baby bunnies!
They are pink!" Her mother folds the wet cloth lengthwise

three times and drapes it over the long silver faucet. She insists
Rachel wear slippers. Together they walk across green lawn

around the trees. When she sees the rabbits tucked so helplessly,
obviously, into a burrow of grass in the middle of the yard,

she tells Rachel, "Don't touch them, honey, so their mother
will come back." And Rachel knows then that she has killed them.

She doesn't tell her mother as they walk hand in hand
through the house's shadow, back up the hill that is only large

because she is so small. Later that afternoon, when she sneaks
out on bare tip toe to look at them once more, the nest is empty.

Her brow creases. She peers across the taller grasses beyond the edge
of lawn but can't see down deep. She studies the roots of the trees.

They are nowhere. Twenty-nine years later, three days
after Rachel's little sister dies of cancer, and before she is lowered

into a water-filled grave, her mother drives away. The mud
is carpeted with two long rectangles of perfect sod. Driving

past the old house with her three children, Rachel sees the hill
is only a gentle slope, though it once went down forever.

Little Rachel Dreams of Regeneration

In third grade,
I read *Pets in a Jar*
cover to cover,
renewed it for weeks
or maybe months,
until the librarian
reminded me other
kids might like it too.
For the rest of childhood
into my teens,
I sought planarians
in wet ditches
and culvert weeds,
scooped jars of murky water
from neighborhood ponds
crouched in cattail reeds.
I never found one,
would never know
if I had courage enough
to slit its funny face
between the eyes
and split its tail
into a fork to watch
it heal into a living
double-headed X,
or better yet, or worse,
a tiny headless man
with two legs, two arms,
two faces for hands,
four tiny, forgiving
eyes, now twice as wise
thanks to me.

The Story Goes

Did you ever cry, Granny, as a tiny girl, an old woman,
missing your missing father—sun-stroked in an Illinois field,
so the story goes, and never quite the same (tap the head)
after that. Or torn by some disorder without that helpful word—
found by grandkids in a 1950 census to have spent four decades
behind security hospital bars, having once thrown a man
down a flight of stairs, declared criminally insane. (*Dead*,
you told your sons, *my father died when I was young*). It is not
your lie but truth that feeds my terror. Did you decide
to spare your boys that swallowed pain, that shame,
stoic, your mouth ever turning a cheek to their kisses,
to ours, no granddad for them to speak of? Did they know?
Or did you simply fear his seed in them and pray for drought.

Pregnant with my father, holding the hand of a toddler,
did you watch your husband, lost inside, exhausted,
drive off past the last gasp of the Great Depression?
Did he truly leave you three for California gold
as you always told them: that no good S.O.B.,
the family refrain? Did you know he later claimed
he tried to see them but was told to stay away
by your husband? *Your sons don't need you*, I imagine
you spat like bloody teeth from the door frame.
They think you nothing but a no good S.O.B. So, he gave up.
You changed Dad's middle and last name to match
his new father's, a gentle dairy farmer, who saved them,
like my stepfather saved me, made them tough.
Thank you. If only erasing a father's name were enough.

I want to think you did it all to stop the secret crying,
so young, so old, the way I did, the way I spent a lifetime
trying to matter to your son after he left us four kids
for his own 70s gold: freedom on a yellow-striped road,
a nurse's bed—that rumor sent through a slant-lit phone
that shrank my mother down to a mute claw. Still,

I didn't escape my father's wily thread: left husbands,
too, for more, for more. Gave up on marriage to live.
Those years I loved him best, Granny, bested him,
your ex and your dad, too. (I wish I knew. I wish I knew.)

My kids would never miss their fathers, never long for me.
We fill the emptiness inside each other like nesting dolls,
seeking, never finding, the smallest nor largest doll—
that ancient animal one that holds or is the core
of us all—nor even the doll we are, just sensing that tiny,
receding, insatiable hole, as if it were only ours.

A Drift of Pigs

In the clearing past the woods
behind our neighborhood, we found
a shot-up car, glass dangling from the
gaping windshield like broken teeth,
a half burnt farmhouse with canned goods
and fruit preserves still on basement shelves
and outdated, thin cotton dresses in the closet

An abandoned barn—full of straw
and a lazy rope—surrounded by a fenced yard
of wild grass and weeds needled through two
jerkified pigs, whiskered leather and teeth
eyes shrunken black

Squeals and groans
slow motion survey of the strange scene
tiptoeing through awful weeds

Who left you in the yard?
Was the farmer's wife crying?
What is it like to die naked beneath the sky?
Was it night?
Were you hungry?

Yellow spread light across me,
my best friends and the pigs like butter

We moved from mundane death mystery
to the stubborn barn door,
ran through the maze of stalls rich
with sweet old stink

Forgetting unlucky pigs, numb
or, perhaps, reveling in our living limbs
despite the pigs, we took turns

with the thick rotting rope, leaped
from the loft and swung
from rafters like promise
after promise after promise, flying,
falling into straw, newborn pigs
stunned by air and gravity
looking up into dust riding light

The Old Phones

The old phones were family pets,
shared, oily, of heft, a comfort,
yet also retractable weapons
you could chuck at your sister,
black her eye and reel in
like a slick catfish. Yes, they were
small, warm bodies or, at least, body parts,
you could innocently fondle, a young cat
cradled against your neck with spiral tail
you could wrap around yourself
a dozen times, a DNA boa, a fetus
whose umbilical cord could stretch
across the kitchen, down the stairs,
through the hall, pulse invisibly under
your door where you could wait forever
on the floor for that boy to say something
into the dark shell of your ear floating
inside the flowered womb of your plush
carpeted bedroom. You could listen
to his busy signal, the silence inside
his steady breathing, all heart
beats. You could hear the voice
of your mother in the distance,
humming receive, receive, receive.

I Can Never be 16 Again & Wouldn't Want to

Though there was that boy with Florida
Eyes who listened to strange, blue
Music yet smiled like a guiltless child.
A child with muscles, cool tennis shoes.
Football player, track runner, woods walker.
Rain chased him everywhere, across fields,
Over water. He couldn't escape. Neither could I.
Not on the sailboat on Lake Springfield
Where we fell asleep, ever virgins, prom night.
Not in his dad's blue-black corvette, hugging
Back road curves through corn to Riverton.
Not in the woods on our backs looking up
Into yellow leafed hearts of giant oaks.
Not in the catfish slip of the Sangamon,
Dangling legs daring the river-cut cliff.
Not in my basement's windowless dark
Where an endless kiss could end in salt.
And it did. We did. On the frontage road
Witnessed by headlights and stars.
I couldn't hold the bruised cloud of him.
He drifted off, past Tallahassee, Atlanta,
Over the panhandle, casting a shadow
The shape of a boy all the way to Illinois.

My Sister's Arm

As little girls
and teens, it was
our favorite sister trick
to trade skin,
so simple to sit
on the sofa,
open my right hand
palm-up on her lap,
her left hand open
palm-up on mine,
arms crossed
in the X of a kiss,
of a chromosome,
the tip of my left finger
perched on her wrist,
her right fingertip
perched on mine.

Eyes closed,
synchronized so as not
to break the spell,
we would slide
our touch slowly, slowly
toward the tender
inner elbow of the other
and back to the wrist
when it would happen:
the eerie sensation
my sister's arm was mine,
her finger now my finger
stroking my own arm
back and forth,
until we could no longer
bear the awful squirm,
the skin-crawling

truth, that future lie:
we are one—
my arm buried with her
in the mud
when she died,
her arm here
begging for touch
as I type.

To My Little Sister, Dying

When it all started to slip,
you crumbled on the overstuffed sofa and cried,
My hands look so old. Saliva stretched across
the quiet chasm of your mouth. Sobs stormed through.
I reached for you, crumbling too, trying to shake
the feeling you believed your life
was not what it was supposed to be,
that your husbands and your church didn't deliver
what you were promised if you were good
(which you were not, you wearily presumed).
And so you took what you got
from doctors and priests in dark suits
and it was not enough to heal you.

Blazing, I desperately willed my muscled love enough
to shine on all your night secrets and patriarchal shame
with such brilliant unflinching beams
that tumors would turn
from your flesh toward my light and evaporate
like water in a stagnant desert puddle. I, too, am naive,
to think I could reach into such rock sheltered shadow,
undo or improve the gorgeous geology of your being.

How could I move the craggy Utah bulges,
shift the polished slots of sky above your callused years
of fear of not attaining celestial glory, salve
the endless pinpricks of husbandly, venereal betrayals,
ease the guilty infidelities of your throbbing
wanting more than disease or dependency from
the men for whom you saved your lust and mud.

Can any sister do this for her sister? I wanted to.
My blood cried for it, but I am not light or even wind!
Our curving walls are too bent to bend light around,

and the wind just carves us deeper. So I am lost
in endless slot canyons, crouching here,
in the shade, in your hand. I won't budge.
When you leave these rocks behind
and your cloudy eyes suddenly soften into shine,
may the innocence of your stubborn love finally
rise from the pores of your hands like vapor,
prismatic through the sky, casting paths of wet light.

2

The Shell

A mother lost in mothering
Ran by the sea. A small girl, perhaps five,
Ran ahead of her. The brown striped shell,
A triton, lay lodged in the shore.
Wet sand sucked at the shell in her hand,
Pulling. The mother was sure
It was hers, her gift from the sea,
Calling her out of sacrifice like a horn.
"Look what the sea gave me!"
"I saw it first," claimed the girl.
Blind in the deep layer of motherhood,
Newly photophagic, the woman refused
To hand it over like a good mother would.
The child would have to pout.
For thirteen years, the woman kept
The shell on a shelf, reminder
Of her in-winding self, the empty sea
Of her own ear, and didn't budge
When her growing daughter often
Told her who saw the shell first.
The day the girl left home a woman,
The mother packed the shell in her duffel
Like a prayer she would some day hear.

Because My Son Announces *Narnia Trees!* on his Seventh Winter Solstice

Driving across Nebraska
we are witnessed

by a stand, no, a hundred mile strand,
of wizened iced trees.

From every tip, ominously fragile,
sag shining branched veins of glassed light.

I start to slough my skin,
drop muscles, organs, bones like leaves

reveal my nerves and veins,
stand up solid in the sun,

reaching, sagging,
a branched thing, silent and clear.

Kate Chopin's Women

When you can't listen to any more
love songs and the ones in your head

have begun to fade, and your lover has stopped
singing about you, and reticent letters have come

to an end, and your children are seldom
adorable, and your husband only

a friend, disappointment gently gives
way to weightless, faceless grace.

There is nothing to be unmade. Nothing
about which to be jaded. Nothing

from which to run. Nothing
for which to wait. Unsolved,

you just stay. Watch
the day. Play at words.

Maybe pray to recall
how to love in this strange

place, or at the edge
of your mind, swim away.

An Eight Year Old Boy

sobs *I hate my life* one hundred and eight times
on his top bunk, refusing touch,
and mother leaves his side after trying
to lie beside him, and father lifts his head
from folded arms to let her climb down the ladder.
The boy eventually sighs himself to sleep
while the parents lie in bed almost holding each other
in the dark, speaking in bed tones of how to best inhale
suffering and exhale relief. She says she wrinkles
her brow, closes her eyes, hunches, feels *red heat*
when she breathes in; opens her eyes, softens
her expression, straightens her shoulders, sees
cool green when she breathes out, because
it is the body that remembers before the mind,
the body where suffering lodges like a sliver
of glass in the palm. It won't work its way out.
He nods. You have to break the skin.

Walk

On the sage straddled trail, green and brown shards perform an earthen version of stained glass windows. Before the path goes black with smelting slag, I let him off leash, stuff it dangling from my back pocket. Leo, the Aussie mystery mix, free to roam, walks beside me, looks up for approval from my left, as if to say, *See, I am good*, until the wind pulls him by the nose here and there, and he stops to drop his drops upon the world, his yellow approval, his self assertion: *I am here*. Even emptied, still he tries. He weaves ahead and back a dozen times, a weft between us. I sing his name—his favorite word, followed by an even better one, the one that makes him tremble, shout in Dog his best English in the family room: *Walk! Walk! Wao-aao-aaao-lk!* I sing both words, for maximum effect, to see him moved: "Leo and Mama goin' on a walk, walk walk, walk walk!" and he begins to dance, circle me, tongue-smiling, prancing, passing behind my legs. I wind him up with happy staccato, "Walk walk, walk walk," dancing myself now, snapping my fingers. He tosses his head against the swinging leash, snatches at it with his mouth, steals it from my pocket. Something dawns. I laugh, he pauses, waits for me to hook his collar, reaches back, takes control of the leash with his teeth, yanks me holding the other end. We walk in the joy of being tied together, our mutual tether. I sing and sing our names. Our feet lift dust. We walk each other. *Walk*, his word for love, the leash between us worn and red.

Picking Up Sons in a Parking Lot

Misunderstanding
the concept "kennel,"
a boy cries quietly
into tissue for three hours
in a car when he believes
his parents are planning
to sell his dog
before holiday travel.
He won't tell his mother
who pleads gently
to know the reason for his tears.
She makes guesses.
He shakes his head.
She wonders if he is protecting her
from her own imperfection.
She is sure it is her fault.
The divorce wound,
the one he will hide
the way she has hid hers
for thirty-five years.
Perhaps he doesn't tell her
he cries for the dog
because he has already
learned that sometimes,
no matter how he feels,
events, decisions and love
are out of his realm of control
and it is no use discussing them.

Nests

But for my love and a fat Siamese
My house is usually empty.
But it is Friday. My turn.

Two sons in tow, we play at random words.
Virgin Mary! Revolutionary War!
Elephant dung! Apocalypse! Ear of corn!

Sam, 12, stops, exclaims, What is that? The sun?
And then we know. The moon! Ah, the moon.
His small voice says, It is a golden dome.

A white car holds us.
We hold the moon like a flat stone
To skip across the prairie.

Let's keep playing, he says.
Grey, 15, begins: Monkey scrotum! Rooster comb!
Dental floss! Alien anal probe!

Once home and helloed, Sam builds
A fire surrounded by concrete blocks.
He feeds it hunks of scrap lumber

And wind-bleached tumbleweeds.
Eventually Grey is cold in thin clothes
And, having laughed enough with me, goes.

Sam tells me of the comet in Orion's belt
Hidden in high clouds.
We walk to the side of the house.

Night has finally laid her white egg.
My boy whispers in a voice
That soon will not be a boy's, It is so mysterious.

And it is: how quietly a nest can fill,
How quickly we can find
Ourselves alone in it.

After the Roast, Advice to an Angry Son

If your children ever ask you,
Have you ever…
They don't want the truth, but do.
Honesty is not the same as love.

But should you feel compelled
To someday tell them how you've flown,
Where you roost, be sure to choose
Today's mistakes like eggs.

The night may come your son
Will feed them to you rapid-fire,
One by one, just to watch you gorge
and puke up bruise-eyed embryos.

Choked sobs and combed excuses
Will not be enough to redeem you
Or him, or your parents' parents' parents.
In the beginning, the nest got robbed.

Furious, beautiful boy, I know.
This is how we try to straighten up
And fly right, broken and young,
Before our chickens come home.

Bridge

At thirteen, the stubborn plastic tube
of childhood ear infections had to be removed.

In its wake, the healed hole did not close,
stole bird wind and breath hymns. Instead,

Sam learned to drum blast beats, buzz rolls,
crash and snare. He learned the muted world,

to turn without fanfare or shame
his better ear toward a quiet voice.

If we had known how easy healing could be
without major surgery, we'd have done it sooner.

With simple tool, a doctor roughed the edges
of the perforation, made a bleeding wound

of tympanum, and with a common hole punch,
cut a dot of paper thin as cigarette skin.

When she placed it on the ragged hole,
it became a bridge for blood, for hope,

for cells to build themselves a road
over the small chasm. Sound began to cross

at once. Driving home, the radio rushed him.
Overcome, he dialed down brass and bass,

like a solitary monk who hasn't seen a friend
in years first bows from the neck, the waist,

then holds him at arms' length
before the caught breath, the full embrace.

And We Will Bloom

I adore you, seed eater,
Spoke Demeter
From afar
To her daughter
Who, laughing,
Ate the whole
Pomegranate
Splatter-handed
In Seattle,
Her new home
Of fog and rain.
And flame.
Forget seasons.
She won't return—
Hades is no man
Or underworld
But this one,
Where roads steal
And homes burn.
Persephone will enter
With her red-seeded heart,
Her jaws of life,
Her mask,
Her heavy water,
Every breath Demeter
Ever gave her,
And rescue someone else's
Son or daughter
From a new kind of hell.

for Sage

Who am I Now that I have Forgiven You

For not forgiving me, you who danced
My soiled clothes before my face, the terror
Of sheets shattered by machine gun fire.
I have never tattered so thoroughly, son.
In shreds, my fingers gripped the wheel
And breath threaded out in gasps. You shot
Words point blank from the back, your face
In the rear view crushed and wet with rage.
Your brother bowed his head and crumbled
On his lap, his mother stripped before him
Like a stained mattress. There was nothing
I could do but lie there, cold. Curled up like you
Asleep once in my body, I could hardly move.
Only a fly could prod me out of bed. I thought
I had forgiven myself. You raised my dead.
I didn't want to forgive you. The afternoon
You called, broken, your voice a brick apology,
I cried for every confession I ever laid,
Folded like sad stories in your wiry arms,
You who were too young to know when,
Where or how to put them away.

with thanks to Sharon Olds for the title

The Worst

I should forgive you, who perhaps
foresaw the worst that I might do,
and forgave before I could act
~from "To My Mother," Wendell Berry

The pistol in the dark closet
The bullets in the drawer
Married in your hands,
Identical to mine but for size,
The taut skin of your youth
And my midlife crevasses.
Already, I have forgiven you,
Forgiven my own imagining
Of your pacing through rooms,
The cold steel of your father's .357,
The dog watching, helpless
While you practiced right angles,
Pressing death against your temple,
Palette, thrusted chin. I have forgiven
The worst you could do before
You did not do it, could not do it.
Even crumbling under the weight
Of morning, your hands,
Built by my blood, reached for a phone
And called two men to come.
Forgive me. The day you were born,
I had already forgiven your reluctant relief
Handing over the gun.

How Often Do You Check on a Sleeping Baby?

Weeks, I woke
in the dark attic room
held my breath
or shuffled blind
hands before me
searching corners
navigating the wake
of a sharp-sloped roof
to his bedside
to listen to him breathe—
my boy on the cusp
of the loaded void
or seventeen.

Moving Home

Perhaps my home
    Is only one inch away,
A shift by which
    I lay my happy self
Upon my unhappy self
    Like a silk screen
Just off register,
    So my edge blurs,
And my sight blurs,
    And my colors breach
Their borders like marks
    Of an errant child,
And the place I live
    Becomes new
Because I am,
    Because I have
Learned a new way
    To move home.

The Mississippi of Motherhood

In the midst of rhapsodizing endless lost days spent at home with my children as babes, toddlers, kids—their faces terrifying lights of innocence looking up, trusting I'd give everything, which I mostly willingly did—those days before a black hole swallowed my resolve, my bed, my home, and finding myself now sitting with my 15 year old son, the baby, who's lived with his father for years, watching the movie he chose, *Colossal*—not one I would choose, but touched, nonetheless, he wanted to watch it with me, knowing I'd like the fight sequences, which I mostly did—I am reminded of the Romantic sublime inside the silence of mothering, those eternal minutes, swept up in children rivers, not drowning, no resting, no branches, no bottom, just treading in place yet moving by giant steadfast current, no white water thrill, just slow and brown, the Mississippi of motherhood, water in my ears, shore out of sight, I could never fully surrender to the pull, nor to the brown depth, and yet, with only three years left in my last child's childhood, I can think of no other timelessness I'd fancy more than the terrifying boredom of slow witness: the mystery of my boy's voice cracking into man, his whiskers, his leg and armpit hairs thickening by the minute. Please, life, I beg: take my remorse, mundane me to bliss, trade me my every regret for this.

Walking the Green Belt

Crestone's piñon desert paths remember
All our feet until the wind.

Post office bound, his dog ahead sniffing the way,
I swear I see my son's size ten Converse tread

Of yesterday, homeward bound from school,
Slightly off the choppy sea of dog paws

And mule deer hooves, the scattered
Patterns of factory made soles in sand.

Imagining his solitary walk, I grin: his cheeks
Rosy with winter, blue eyes scanning

For prickly pear, then, the sudden upward glance
At sky, his left foot stepping just there.

This His First Night Drive

After the movie, driving home from Alamosa,
I pulled off Highway 17 so we could swap seats.
My son—newly permitted, this his first night drive—
Clutched the wheel tightly at ten and two o'clock.
Tense? I asked. *I'm nervous,* he replied. *Why?*
All these bunnies on both sides of the road!
Sure enough, there they were—every few yards,
Ears poked up in tufts of grasses I had overlooked,
Giant desert jackrabbits peering out in silhouette,
Perfect profiles of chocolate bunnies, ears perked.
Prolific— no wonder they are Easter's mascot.
Farther down, more and more, their lumped corpses
Littered the road, unable to rise from the dead
Except as wings, promising a veritable buffet
For morning's magpies. (A memory: we almost
named him Corvidae.) Poor Sam, I thought,
As knowledge of this deadly power dawned on him.
First, he dropped his speed. Then, this boy, who
Hasn't yet discarded childhood's matted teddy bears,
Who shares a bed with his old dog, began to practice
The fast stop, brakes slammed just enough to save us all.

3

Calculating a New Vocabulary of Joy

We multiply families of ravens,
stun words in cool gusts,
then lift, winged heat. I ramble
mathematically, waiting for a language,
croaking, ready to give up everything tertiary.

What primal number,
what rough cut square footage
expresses itself in our shared gaze?

What equals one mountain plus one man plus one woman
plus three habaneros sliced thinly, coughing steam,
sex and gasoline, gratitude dividing
into soft apologies to one tree for sinking nails
that hold prayer flags and all sentient beings?

How do two people become
one home in a flash? Quite simply.
The sky calculates it all like this:

One crisp ponderosa accepts you. I notice.
We sniff its neck. The moon squints
though its 2 am limbs upon our tangled sleep.
One cabin, our larger body, stirs
under twenty fingers. Its engine spills and fumes.

A decomposing granite hallway
takes our four-legged gait like seed,
grunts us new. Like this, teeth smiling.

We might be two parallel streams and the earth
is giving way between.
We can't account rationally for the speed
of our lives' glorious destruction
or the volume of water tearing through.

The solution is in the weep, the wound,
the rocky crack. Guess how
the clever juniper grew where it grew.

Tiny Birds

Beaks buried in nectar,
Bodies buddhas,
Wings blur.

We study throats,
Rusty bellies
In books, windows.

My grandmother's words
Were once full
Of hummingbirds.

Last night, every time
We kissed, one
Burned inside my dark mind.

When the feeder tips,
The tiny bird
Moves with it.

This is Not a Test

1. Stepping out of the car at the Comfort Inn,
We watched my Mormon father
Cross the parking lot.
    a. Each man grew a comb in the closing distance.
    b. Palm to palm with a Black man, Dad looked up.
    c. Suspicions about my partner's name: confirmed.
    d. One neck throbbed harder.
    e. All or none of the above.

2. In Maverick's Country Grill
Over roast and mashed potatoes,
Dad called Dorell a big boy.
    a. Boy, of course, meant youth, and "Welcome, son."
    b. His mother's grandfather's will bequeathed a man to a man.
    c. His wife didn't kick him under the table.
    d. Dorell held my father's eyes and smiled outside of time.
    e. All or none of the above.

3. When we sat in the dim hotel room
Lit by the screen of perpetual cowboy westerns,
My father and I, surprised, choked up in patriotic pride.
    a. Which America made him cry?
    b. Did he notice our fingers laced with Dorell's like keys?
    c. "America the Beautiful" rang from our palms.
    d. He didn't know he would stop his monthly phone call.
    e. All or none of the above.

after A.E. Stallings

The Carpenter

You did not give me life,
But, in choosing her and four of us,
Showed me how love lives
Inside a man when he enfolds
A small girl's mother in the pause
Of making dinner in a kitchen,
Or calls her My Bride,
A smile in the way he says
Her names, first and middle,
Rocking her to the quiet song
Of the pressure cooker's
Clicking weight spurting steam.
When we ate, my mother
Served you first.
When she laid down the law,
Your posture—voice calm and firm—
Made us honor her.

A grown woman now, I know:
You did not have to.

You did not have to teach me
How to tie a knot with seven twists,
Hold down fins with a tight grip
To gently pull a hook,
Nor gut, nor skillfully filet a fish.
You did not have to cut a door
For my dog into the shed you built
Nor give her straw for a bed
Nor build a cable run.
You did not have to lend me tools
To make an elephant of a dowel
Nor bet it was impossible
Nor grin and give me a dollar
When I proved you wrong.
You did not have to sing to me
Of pretty bubbles in your pick-up
Nor teach me the joy of ridiculous riddles
Whose answers' only sense is to laugh.

You did not have to take us—
Take us to the lake to water ski,
Nor thrill us with the roaring outboard,
Sink the stern with speed
To lift us, perched upon the bow,
Children skyward thrown.
You did not have to teach me
Water's words: port and starboard.
You did not have to wake first
After a night of steady rain
To make us bacon, mush and eggs
While we slept in sagging tents.
You did not have to cry
When my sisters and I sang hymns
Nor hold my hand with your rough one—
Fragrant with Corn Husker's lotion,
Watching sitcoms on the couch.

You did not have to.

You could not have known
Thirty years later I would see
A carpenter's pencil—sharpened,
Like yours, into facets with a knife,
Resting flat on my love's handmade cabinet,
Waiting for his pocket, its lead scent
Praying for the wooden day to begin—
And a deep joy would rise in me
Remembering my true father,
The carpenter who built
A home in me for this.

for Lahne

Anatomy of a Mason Jar

First you were for cucumbers,
The bread and butter pickles
I taught him to love, their yellow
Stain brightening his egg salad.

Or was it beets, the obscene
Lolling eyeballs of earth. Red.
Your glass a lantern full
Of cloved, impossible sight.

It doesn't matter. Rusted ring, lost lid,
You have outlasted better glasses
In the cabinet, crystal goblets,
Cheap tumblers, stately beer pints.

You are our finest, my pride,
For serving guests wine despite
Hard water marks on your shoulders,
White mineral threads along your neck.

Humble belly of water, tattooed
Name in raised script, you are the vessel
At my bedside, the three a.m.
Wide mouth against parched lips.

Settling back into the down,
When he hands you to me
In the prairie dark of dawn,
You are his clear promise.

American Gothic Koan

How many cicada midnights
in the history of hotwired pastures
love and basketball

have a black man and a white woman
shot bent hoops with a spilt egg moon
off a Farmall tractor?

On Chickens: A Pastiche

Small town Illinois girl, once London-lost,
now Colorado-, I feed chickens
plastic-packaged crumble. Crumbled what?
It's non-organic. Half the cost.
It worries me I can't afford to do the right thing.[1]
It's winter. Foraging is over. Grasshoppers live
in my omelet even when I forget every bone
and bird and worm has spirit in it.[2]
What spirit lives in crumble?

Other times, excruciatingly alive,[3] I flinch.
Once, a white local rancher/our new landlord
told my man (must you know he's Black?)
The previous tenant—white trash—
nigger-rigged the bathroom plumbing.
We didn't say a thing, just blinked.
Later, chewing chicken fajitas, he laughed,
Maybe I'll just Digger-rig* it. He didn't say,
Cast down your bucket where you are,[4]
though this is what he has to do. Unruffled,
Nebraska born, he perfectly plumbed
that bathroom. He didn't say, We wear the mask.[5]
Unemployed, last night he dreamed his legs
were white like mine when he removed his pants
to give them to the homeless San Francisco man.

What does his skin have to do
with mine? Middle aged, I have cried
that we will bear no blackish child[6]
nor have to hide my father's
cherished 19th century will
in which a slave was passed down to a son.
I won't forget my father's gleeful, childhood
march to Beethoven. *Kill the Jews! Kill!*
he dreamed they must have sung.
Or ever hear him say,
Let those I love try to forgive
What I have made.[7]

Instead of eat[ing him] like air,[8]
I [ache] as if he were already gone.[9]
Unlike my solid daughter, I crumble,
feed myself to flightless chickens
I've never had to steal
nor slaughter.

1. Sherman Alexie, "What you Pawn I Will Redeem"
2. Gloria Anzaldua, *Borderlands/La Frontera*
3. Gloria Anzaldua, *Borderlands/La Frontera*
4. Booker T. Washington, "Up from Slavery"
5. Paul Laurence Dunbar, "We Wear the Mask"
6. Gwendolyn Brooks, "A Bronzeville Mother Loiters in Mississippi"
7. Ezra Pound, "CXX"
8. Sylvia Plath, "Lady Lazarus"
9. Alison Bechdel, "Fun Home: A Family Tragicomic"

Shed Dreams

The little shed was a wooden skull
In which the dreams of shovels rusted
And feral cats jumped from shelf to shelf
Chasing brown, white-bellied mice.

Hundreds of generations dreamed
Behind a stack of asbestos shingles—
Of corn meant for hogs, of fantastic forays
To the human house of bounty and heat,

Where heroes lick clean peanut-buttered traps
That snap little necks beneath the kitchen sink.
Less curious mice would tuck their luck
In the shadows of the skull, nibble cat droppings.

Capacious as a mouse's dream, the shed
Never thought of human sleep, that one day
Its roof would lift, its walls would echo nails,
The sun would finally stumble in and cough.

The cats took off. Who knows when mice move out?
The shed began to dream a man, an orange antique couch,
A chair, a bed, a woman dreaming a head made of mud
She saved from her boots, from her sister's grave.

A Year after the Abortion

We thought the leghorn
and Greg Brown no longer laid.
Come look, my lover said.

Nestled in wall insulation,
its paper layer pecked
clear through, lay seven eggs,
four brown, three white
in the back of the shed.

Unsure how long they'd been,
though January and February
probably preserved them,
I smashed them in the run
and fed them to their hens,
who do not mind to peck and pinch
their unborn from the dead.

Free Range Bunny Meets Brer Hare

Trickster tales themselves are tricky; their seriousness is hidden and often overlooked.
~Trudier Harris, "The Trickster in African American Literature"

We let her roam about.
Mornings. Afternoons.
She never wandered past the earth.
Dug shady holes in which to rest
From summer heat.
Come dusk, I laughed
As he chased her in a stuttered dance.
Big black man. Fat grey bunny.
Catching her came easier to me.

We fed her pellets, carrots, wilted lettuce.
Thoughtful family economist,
He planned to one day breed her
For cost-effective meat, flavorful and lean.
Resigned, preparing, I once dreamed
He broke a rabbit's neck, his own neck
Tenderly inclined, while standing in the sea.

Young chickens loved to taunt
And bully her with bobbing beaks,
Lay eggs in the yawning hutch
While she was out. She handled hens
With expert dart and speed.

Once I caught her nose-to-nose
With a wild hare.
Would you like to call him Brer?
We watched them trade full chase
In wide, shifting spirals.
The rancher warned, was right:
Bunny caught Brer's fleas.
I treated her with powder,
Caged her for over a week.

Finally flea-free, lonely
On her last release, at dusk

She disappeared.
I searched her usual haunts.
Pile of siding. Propane tank.
Nose twitching, Brer Hare stared at me.
Dorell, unsurprised,
Shrugged, his mouth set in sympathy:
Raccoon must've carried her off.
We lived a few more weeks.
Sometimes, I thought I caught her
On the breeze.

Yesterday, he found her near the hives
Where weeds are tall as men.
Rich puddle of grey fur
Like cattail down set free,
Vibrating with black crawling beneath.
The only signs of architecture:
One leg bone, bare, pointing at sky.
Spinal column, clean, disembodied
As though hand-laid
By the writhing, silken pelt.
No head to speak of.
I used to kiss her cheek.

(Is it too much to add, to say?):
Today I found Brer Hare
Freshly dead on the edge
Of our drive, hit and thrown
Off the county road
He was bold enough to dare.

Join me, will you, while I try
Not to make a mess, not to cry
Not to make this story mine
Nor metaphorically align
Nor signify.

People are not hares.

after the murder of Philando Castile

Walking the Pasture

The night we walked
the two-pathed road—the one
you accidentally carved
in the pasture driving buckets
of corn and water drawn warm
from our winter bathtub
back and forth to three pigs
who skip and snort every time
your silver pickup climbs
the gentle hill and stops—
the farm light, as always, took over
where the moon left off.
Clouds crept in from the east.
We smelled but doubted rain.
We smiled but doubted this, our place.
Orion, in his simplicity,
pinpoints of restlessness shining,
hunted the western horizon
without finding it, shoulders lit,
chest filled with night.

Building

A couple walks
into a house and knows
it is the one.
For years they
will bend it
and each other
toward
the life they want.

Around beds
of irises and echinacea
her gully rocks doze.
His callouses raise
walls for chickens,
basil, arugula,
pour a foundation,
puzzle together
a dome.

Her toddler task:
hand up
triangular panes
of glass one by one
and wait
until he is done
with other
buildings paying
bills, feeding children.

Their silent fights
could fell a pine,
peel a porch,
invent new words.
Their tenderness
could birth a
sutra, decades,
this church.

Outside the Path of Totality

I never knew my hands were cameras,
Their tiny spaces human pinholes
Of Renaissance technology,
Projecting what is upside down
To trace the world's lines.

Unable to look up,
I filter bitten sun through fingers.

How did we get here? This point
Where men no longer fear
Gods will steal the day forever for our hate,
Marching through streets with torches,
Effigies of burning crosses, effigies
Of black bodies flaming in leaves.

Even the leaves of lynch trees
Become apertures.
How dare you strive to turn the oak
Against the sun?

Countless crescent suns
Shimmer in astonishing shadows at our feet.

Black feet of the man I love—
Warped with work and callouses,
Black feet I have rubbed with oil,
Touched with lips, toenails like moons,
Their clippings, eclipsed suns—
Walk this earth.

That day in a pause at work,
He took a photo of tree shadows
To give me all the smiling suns,
Sent it through air to me
Taking the same picture to send to him
In the pause of my own day,
Nudging students to care, to see,
Say something.

How dare you strive to turn the trees
Against this love?
We cannot be obscured.
Our eyes are moons and suns at once.
Arms wrap around each other's sore backs,
Black hands warm on white skin,
White hands warm on black,
Who is eclipsing whom? No one.

We are love, unstoppable phenomenon.

One student called it awesome and awful.
We have no control of it. Heatless light.
Another called it midday dusk and dawn.

Take off your cardboard glasses.
Drop your eyes to earth.
Bless light filtering trees.
Look through your own hands
And weep at what you have done.

after the Unite the Right white supremacist rally in Charlottesville, VA, and the following total solar eclipse

The Closest Ones the Brightest

On a day of domestic nouns, undecorated,
This Christmas refuses to go retrograde
Or snooze through the moment by resurrecting
High-buzzing toy trains or the forsythia bush
I planted when my sister died. My nostrils
Did not flare in sorrow over chemo anecdotes.
Sunlight yellowed only the mountain range.
Wrapped in a blanket, feet propped on the porch,
I slipped into a micro nap and woke to coyotes
Broadcasting the new minutes of evening.
Juncos flitted behind me in the pines.
Later, walking piñon trails of moon-lost night,
Strange flashlight throwing sight forward
And back at once to warn our single-filed feet
Of stones, I thought of red clay, the joyful skill
I find my fingers still possess, of gently pinching,
Smoothing shoulders, clavicles, muscled necks,
Of fashioning tiny human forms for company,
Of Nu Wa, Chinese goddess, who carefully molded
The noble from yellow earth and, tiring,
Gave up to make the poor by dipping a rope
In mud and flicking it about, dropping dollops
Of common folk, elbows bent to serve.
Thank gods the thick Milky Way sparkled me
Out of my head and cold thighs itched me
Out of Marxist bitterness because my dog was
Out of town, not stitching me with dog bliss
To the night, the sandy mountain trail all his.
Only my man was by my side, quiet, digesting
Chili and cinnamon rolls, both of us making
Walking sounds, his boots clicking, my jacket
Swishing, both of us squinting at headlights
Crawling up T Road, heading our way, gaining
Elevation, the closest ones the brightest.

Abide

Rufous-Sided Towhee

Eastern and Spotted Towhee have each been restored to full species status; formerly considered one species, Rufous-sided Towhee. The two interbreed along rivers in the Great Plains, particularly the Platte and its tributaries.
~from National Geographic Field Guide to the Birds of North America

Chub chub zee, the bird says, while I dig grass out of garden mornings. Chub chub zee. I know at once I once knew the bird's name. I wait days for it to come. Too far gone. Google offers only sex slang and a rapper's name. Finally, I text my boys' father who taught me its song twenty years ago when we were in love. What bird says Chub chub zee? *Spotted Towhee*, he texts back, *Remember them in Escalante?* I do not. *They have a red eye!* And later, when Grace stops by to help me identify a weed, she explains the bird used to be called Rufous-Sided Towhee. Yes, that's it! The bell rings. "It's too bad," she ponders, "it was more fun to say." A sadness flies inside. Like tiny Pluto of my youth, someone decides to reclassify a planet, a species, and the world accepts a new truth. Publishers update field guides, birders comply, but Spotted Towhee will never ring in me. "Drink your tea," Grace says the bird sings, or simply, "Drink tea," but it isn't her voice. It is his, drawing out and trilling "tea," and our boys' high-pitched throats in mimicry, giggling. Memory opens like morning sky. I mourn the Rufous-Sided Towhee.

What We Could Not Let Go Of

It is the time my father's voice
Begins to slur; my mother's back and blood
Cannot move her, move slowly enough through her,
Without a knife, a pill, a corpse's generous bone.
Death is not her friend but his, with its habit
Of gifting what is left of close and distant
Relatives. He never wastes a breath
On Death's ill-timed greed.

He asked my dying sister Becca
For her new red Ford to give his favorite son.
She must have boiled to save it for her husband.
Thwarted even so, Death is not my father's foe.
How else would he have made a life
Pulling the maimed from cars
Crushed by speed, houses charred
By pretty lights? It is all matter of fact.

My mother, though, is still a glass
Full of her daughter's final glassy stare.
Every night she shatters sleep
With too long prayer and careful notes
On kitchen counters to be read
By the living and the dead in looping script.
Rebecca, I love you! last night's note said.
Having just arrived alive by plane, I wasn't jealous.

My own young sons already walk the house, divvy up
Their father's guns, guitars, his father's army
Knives. "Vultures," he laughs. Perhaps.
Their urge is just as natural as burial in the sky.
The birds fly off with eyes and arms.
Our things, our larger bodies,
Feed our young what we once loved,
What we could not let go of.

Sempervivum

I break off last year's surprising stalks, sprouted
like prehistoric towers from mother-centered clusters
of hens and chicks, and drop them in the bare spots
of the rock garden. The rosette from which each stalk grew
is absolutely dead. I do not know if her brown blooms
have already thrown chick seeds or if chicks simply move
like my succulent babes, sending runners underground.

One Friday Morning

Exactly one week after a young man drops
three feet to the ground from a piñon branch,
landing—his mother imagines in quiet horror—on all fours,
crouched like his childhood superhero, one hand
pushing himself up in slow motion, the other rubbing
his throat, coughing, gasping, eyes watering
as he begins the walk home, hoodie pulled tight,
stars winking forever behind the gibbous moon,

she is dragging crushed cardboard pizza boxes
and five bags of household waste—two of which
she has marked with T in red permanent ink,
the other three with R—to the end
of the grey gravel drive under the piñon.
With clear packing tape, she attaches to one bag
a $30 check in a business sized envelope on which
she has written Thanks to the thin local man
who picks up the bags with his van every week.
An hour passes before she realizes it is not Monday.

Against weekend bears, she carries the bags back
to the storage shed, sees the beer box on a shelf
she has filled with kitchen knives, painkillers,
flu meds, scissors, extension cords, hammock
straps. Gently closing the door, she turns a key
in the padlock. Thinks of where to put her keys.
Catching her breath, stepping out from the car port,
pacing the drive in no specific direction, she notices
Russian sage, the bright rising mist, scans the forest
at the foot of the Sangre de Cristo mountains,
now indebted forever to the unknown tree,
unable to untie her son's broken hope from its limb.

Milky Way

Silvia Barajas-Ceja once said,
"No bad thoughts while you bake
Or you'll ruin the cake," but I mixed
An inexplicable sadness in with the eggs,
And the cake baked just fine,
Except for when it sank a bit when I opened
The door too early. Undaunted, sadness
Rose again like a chest after inhalation,
Goldened and fell again, cooling
On the stovetop. It didn't matter.
You flip a three-milk cake upside down
Anyway, and it should look flat,
Not domed. When my knife shagged
The wall of the cake and left a gouge
Right before I dropped it on the plate,
I didn't care. Whipped cream hides
The dents, swaddles my sorrow
Like baby Jesus to feed my friends.
When they said it was the best cake
They'd ever had, my sorrow
Sparkled in their eyes, a milky way.

Undraped

A domestic Christo and Jean Claude,
I let dust, coiled hairs, black grounds,
bread crumbs and toothpaste puddle crusts
drape my surfaces like white or pink fabric,
orange and blue umbrellas only I can see
across the landscapes of my house. I notice,
I notice, the textured grime, the tiny piles
of things. Days may pass, or weeks, until
I cannot bear anymore the memory, suspense
of what's underneath—abstract shapes, clean
lines, order, shine revealed by spray or sponge.
I become the artist and the audience in one,
for those who do not notice what needs wiped,
do not notice it newly bright, except perhaps
in an unexpected lightness of mood while
stirring coffee before setting down the spoon.

The Guitar

A guitar watches a blue boy
play video games all day.
Its blind eye does not blink.
He cannot think of school.
Strings vibrate when he
laughs in vanished victory,
groans in bloodless defeat.
Xs shine in his eyes, ask
Why do anything?
The guitar has no reply.

D-Con

We found his box of green pellets, stuffed
the poison in our cheeks, carried it away
to a high place out of reach of the children:
a plastic bag of pillows dangling from a top bunk.
We tried not to swallow en route, leapt the chasm,
made a dozen deadly deposits in the pillows,
hoped against hope the toxic dust would not
dry us up, turn our blood against our own hearts.
In the meantime, in the daily hurried rituals
of scurry, gather and hide, barely sleeping,
we forgot where we tucked away our riches.
When it snowed, a woman found our pine nuts
in her snow boot. When she spilled her coffee,
grass seeds cached in towels high on a shelf
spilled out like confetti into her mouth. The next day,
stuck to threads of a cotton nest chewed into a mattress
pad stored under the bed, she found our mother
a brown, dried horror husk, mealworms long dead
in the small bowl of her skull, the ribs of her chest.

circa Trump's defeat

Late Blooming

To decide if you need to buy tomatoes, you visit yours.
One rots on the rock upon which you propped it
to avoid moist soil. Prehistoric armored insects
encircle it like centuries, or sentries, overseeing its
slouch, its decay, waiting their turn. Nearby, volunteer
marigolds riot gold despite blighted potato leaves,
freckled black. There may be nothing underground.

Nearby in another bed, mixed greens and red
nasturtiums flourish with volunteer snap peas
still wearing their purple hats, climbing
gone-to-seed arugula. And here, more volunteer
marigolds outlive their curly-seeded cousins, calendula,
offer shade to yellow-tongued violets' small bloomings.
You couldn't have anticipated these fall palettes:
complementary, analogous, too pretty, too tough to eat.

Nearby, a hammock of similar hues hangs between two
piñon trunks on straps that recently have come to mean
unfathomable lethality to your thought-hewn son.
You must take the hammock down. You try to shake
off grief. You shake needles from the woven cloth,
lay in it beneath the branches, swing in your cradle.
Somehow, in the dapple, you decide to trust
his wooden wisdom, fate-earned, your dark Odin
who survived his own terrible world tree.

My Mother's Geraniums

It is safe to write about red geraniums,
their sharp, earthy aroma, and imagine them,
once summer and hummingbirds have passed,
dragged in off the porch, blooming indoors
all winter like my mother's prayers, so red,
such bright fistfuls of love for her wounded ones,
it is hard not to think of blood, her blood pumping
through all of us, if it could, if she could will it.

False Metaphor

For months a mother
fell, and fell, felt sorry
for the forest,
sighed apologies to trees.

The thought of her son
climbing one of its
gentle trunks
to leap into
the lowest share of sky
felt somehow like she
by benevolent neglect
betrayed the forest,
released a tight fist
of seeds too soon.

Her green pinecone.
Her own sorrow stones
passed on unwittingly,
dropped early,
too raw to root.
False metaphor.

She sees now in the sag
and hears in drips
of late winter snow,
walking through
a gentle piñon grove,
that it is the forest
who felt sorry first
for him, for her, and broke
with love to save
them both from air.

Feeding My Father

in our age or in theirs or in their deaths
saying it to them or not saying it —
if we forgive our fathers what is left
~from "forgiving our fathers," by Dick Lourie

When Lewy
bodies in his brain
locked his arm midair,
I lifted the forkful
of eggs to his open lips.

My mouth opened too,
the way mothers' mouths do
while feeding their infants.
The unexpected gift—
I found the truth:

we are all gaping.
I finally forgave him
for forgiving himself
for everything he did
and could not do.

Icon

On what felt like
my life's final night
with my father,
his fast yet failing feet
shuffled to the archway
and lingered,
voice stolen—
a stooped silhouette,
icon backlit by blue light—
to look into the room
where I lay in the dark
on an air mattress,
slowly deflating,
for a last look at me,
his breathing child,
who would
drive away forever
in the morning.

Final Grief

The edgeless hole
you left in my childhood
chest awaits.

I beg life. I beg you.
Let me lower
your body into that grave.

Let me shovel dirt
over every lost and never-made
memory of you.

Let me tuck you into earth
with my story,
hide you like a bone.

I'll lean on my shovel and sob.
Roll out a rectangle of sod.
Lie over you like a dog.

I'll sit up. Stand like sky.
Walk back into my life,
your living tombstone.

Faint Station

…on blood antenna/ and dust radio
~Chris Whitley

On those days
static leans hard
on either side of me,
I'm a song
I no longer hear.
You hold me
in the kitchen,
a dial tuning in
to a sliver. Listen,
this is a faint station.
Never out of range,
you always find it.

for Dorell

Vigil

A blue, white and green
painting hangs over our heads,
large with trying to be water and air
and the space between,
as though three elements could be
simple color and their memory enough
to soothe me in the dark on clean sheets.

Startled awake, my pulse believes
you are the man on screen
stranded in the middle of a road
walking away from death,
helicopter hovering overhead,
disembodied voice seeing just enough
of size and skin to summarize you.

Any move you make to reach for phone,
I.D., risks your body's claim
to blue, white and green.
No last text *I'm on my way*.
From above, at dusk, we don't know
if the pixelated bloom on your shirt
is black or red.

I blink in the dark.
I can't see you.
You breathe, refuse screens.
Pressed against your heat,
I let you sleep.

after the murder of Terence Crutcher

Reteach a Thing its Loveliness

...sometimes it is necessary/ to reteach a thing its loveliness,/
to put a hand on its brow.../ and retell it in words and in touch/
it is lovely/ until it flowers again from within, of self-blessing/
as St. Francis/ put his hand on the creased forehead/ of the sow...
~Galway Kinnell

I'm not sure which I prefer—
a dog-ruined couch
felted with fur and saliva,
my heart unfurled
by that dog's head on my lap,
mother-loneliness ruined
by unblinking brown eyes,
child-starved fingers sated
by silken ears and skull,
his musky scent a welcome
pocket of ancient wilderness
inside my home,

or this clean couch,
spotless but for drips
of coffee here and there,
bread crumbs tucked
in corded seams,
its arms stained
with my arms' oils,
my heart in solitary repose
considering a poem
by Galway Kinnell
called "St. Francis
and the Sow,"
while my dog rests
over there on his bed,
his chin on the low
window sill, peering out,
a palm of morning light
upon his brow.

On Reading Woolf Again after 26 Years

Over Thai, bright eyed, Chrissy confessed
she once wrote out every sentence
Virginia Woolf ever penned.
Novels. Short stories, essays too.
The way the nuns would read
fine literature aloud and pause
as pupils scratched down word
for word in perfect penmanship.
The nuns were, I was, laying down the track,
she said, *for what a sentence could do.*
And now, as I re-read Orlando's thoughts,
Clarissa's— gasp at her shilling tossed
into the Serpentine, her never-Septimus
(Clarissa's double; Woolf's triple, and mine)—
and think them, I am also thinking Chrissy's,
perhaps, marveling at Virginia's odd clauses,
generous commas, semicolon hitches; hooking
coach cars; occupied by well-heeled, awkward
friends; freight cars bursting delphinium;
shadow cargo; centuries of ice coupled
with foiled men waking up as women;
everything pulling on everything else
behind the locomotive of her mind;
riding a rail that will never arrive,
or always; in Vita's arms; in one of several
lakes; in my hands; yours. Call it luck
to rattle under the warping weight of her,
all of us, every place: her station.

for Chrissy Mason, with fondness

To Measure Him

Dozens of number-covered papers
Claim to represent what is vital about my son.
Blood. Knowledge. College readiness. Genes.
Brain chemicals disguised as ambition, anxiety, love.
I study them like runes, riddles, scientific scripture.
What numbers are light blue like his hurt eyes?
Gravelly with laughter over mastered digital dances?
Flushed like his kind face over fragrant cast iron pans?
Steaming with pure hockey joy? Long road silent?
Early to sleep on the family couch, cradled in yarn,
Wrapped in magic arms of a mandala afghan?
Numbers strike as monolingual, unholy arrogance:
This summing up, ridiculous reduction of gentleness,
Unbearable empathy, early existentialism.
It makes more sense to measure him by this:
How many moon eclipses he has witnessed
Just beyond a gasp-shared meteor. One.

Shedding

The antique Iraqi rug likely never knew a family dog
before ours. When I vacuum it after he leaves
for a weekend with my son, it is usually with a sense
of a few days' relief from hair everywhere. On Sundays
when he returns, I don't care that God's woven trails
of geometric red and indigo turn dusty mauve
and grey with down. That is the way with dog hair.
You bear it. But today, when my son packed bags
to live with his dad two hours away and took
with him only a few of the things I gave to give him
small reasons to raise his head, I almost understood.
A mother's love isn't all. Her wisdom is at best, for now,
a suffered fluff. Teenage boys want only a bit of it
and something more: the clutter and berth of freedom
fathers sagely give to man-sized sons. I vacuumed
the rug what felt a final time. I did it sobbing,
drooling, with a knotted grudge. A hunch. My son
will forge his own mind. The dog will not get walked
enough; we both will fatten up. If I had had the time
and foresight to spin, I'd have saved and combed
and spun the past year's every tuft of liver-spotted fur
to knot a musky blanket of the love that dog
has learned nuzzling my son. I'd sleep under it.

Sage's Puja

Having wandered the Lakshmi gift shop
With my daughter Sage, we end
Our ashram tour in the circular temple.
I stop at guru photos and bow, drop a dollar
In a plate, not personally knowing
The special gift or allure of these holy men,
Only their serious, black eyed gaze.
Sage, a newly hired Tacoma firefighter,
Pauses before photos and paintings, too,
Asks, Who is this? The Divine Mother.
And this? Babaji. And here's Shiva, I say,
Knowing she knows his Nataraja form,
Brass dancer engulfed by a ring of fire
Who roamed the bookshelves
And windowsills of her childhood home.
Having walked the solemn perimeter,
This woman who nearly burned down
Her bedroom twice before fully grown
Comes to the fire extinguisher
Near the door, taking its modern place
On a wall of ancient gods and saints.
In slow reverence, she lifts her hand
To touch the words Cold Fire.
Sighing, ignited, she throws a glance
At her firefighter fiancé,
Her smiling mouth beatific, aflame.

Half Mud Half Slush

Trail divided lengthwise, half mud half slush,
each foot struggles with different problems,
like a brain walking a body alone through piñon
while simultaneously overlaying an older scene:

a dog's tail wagging yards ahead and stopping
mid stride to run back to check she is still there,
past and present always gathered beneath her,
beneath each moment like two competing feet.

16 and 19

Taller than   their mother,   now men,
heavy-   hearted heads   their inheritance,
sometimes   they are little boys,   straddle handles
on   rolling suitcases   to ride them,
long legs   Fred Flintstoning   down the ramp
to   plane entrances.   Then they are
holograms: mirages of toddlers,   5- to 12-year-olds
prism-tilting   out at all angles   superimposed over
grown bodies   like time   ghosts.

Ballistics

Twenty years forward
six feet behind
the antique rocker (point one)
in which I nursed
my firstborn son—
a bullet hole in the floor
instead of his head
(the second and third points
of a scalene triangle),
blessed.

Minefields

The moment when a feeling enters the body/
is political. This touch is political/ said Rich*
the year I was born a girl. The minefields

of my husband's Black body, mine,
my sons' white bodies, mine, proliferate.
Text fields. Silent white woman mother wife

poet, keep quiet. (Not) your stories to write. Mine.
My body ignores their borders, knows what lies
beneath a temple, gun, knee, has hung from trees.

Keep them all alive, three hearts beat/en outside
my body, mine, blood I built and build with touch.
I turn down, muffle public words. Cannot speak

for the men I serve, lives, minds (not) mine. Mine.
I tiptoe, tremble, touch their skin, wrap arms
around them in the dark, in the kitchen.

after the murder of George Floyd

Slow Touch

I lie open eyed in the dim morning.
He is finally asleep after another 4 AM waking.
I mostly let him drift, sometimes
interrupt his snore to wrap an arm around,
across him, until decades of ache drive me
back into solitary postures. Hungry, I reach
again, hand seeking the buried beat inside
his silken chest, place a kiss, another,
on his warm shoulder. He sighs the sigh
that comes from slow touch, manages a turn
to lay his heavy arm across my waist, his hand
somewhere in the void beyond me. I wait
for that hand. Only when bored restlessness
and the clock finally win, when I sit up, pause,
feet on the chill floor, does he reach to caress
the small of my back or hip poised to stand.
A small investment. We both know I must go.
Perhaps it is similar to the way I call my mother
when I am driving toward mountains, knowing
I will lose signal soon and the conversation
has a sure expiration, will not wander on for hours,
my mother's retelling tales of loss and longing,
ever etching grooves—waiting to be played, waiting
for the needle to drop—on her daughter's body.

Your River

Smart speakers offer manual options for volume
for people like you whose giggle, talking ridiculously
to plastic, quickly turns to awe and bossiness.
Hey, Google, play "River" by Leon Bridges.

Hey, Google, 75% volume. Hands free, music makes
a soundtrack for cooking, cutting onions. Living.
Hey, Google, 100% volume. Constant visual overlay
these days. Memory's relentless mind screens couple

with memories of small screens, fingers scroll songs,
click video versions: a Black father's blood-spattered
white t-shirt, his baby crying, calmed on his chest, tiny
red-wet fingers, Black people in white, standing in water,

not the literal river you misremember: they sing in rain
enhanced by a hose, join the onion on the cutting board.
This isn't video. Your husband is out buying avocados
and blue chips. The song story thunders through you just

below a rolling memory of the morning he held you up
on your feet, thighs and knees giving out with father grief,
beneath your cry, are you going to leave me?, and the song
came on spontaneously, the river song, the song

now always a stream in the dark of your son's room,
smelling of unwashed clothes and an old dog,
the room, looking into the kitchen, where he, your love,
sat with you on a messy floor-mattress, untangled

antique knots of abandonment, your face a river.
You say you are always waiting for what you deserve,
that being left is what you will get for what you gave
and have been given, your narrative inheritance.

He asks, can't we rewrite that end? I want to, you say.
Songs shuffle. Onions gleam. The kitchen glows yellow
with the promise of a new mythology, a river flowing
without water, without gravity, without a final sea.

Retreat

There stands my child
in no man's land,
a man in no child's land.
Hard to say: mine child
or hologram man, lifting
and flickering every age
from the tilted page of earth.
I shift, pace, calculate
the best route to the other
side past barbs where
lives his enemy—a mirror,
a word, a job, a meal,
a gentle touch, a circle
of sober men talking.
I whisper *retreat*,
worried my voice will trip
the wire in his ear,
the brain, take us both
out. My voice is not
a hologram. I watch,
wordless, beg the cells
of him made half of me
to defuse, to move,
not move, and the silence
is a yellow fog I've
no mask for.

Family Organism

I want to say, please see
your arms and smile my back
my hours your broken strut
your roof my road to sleep
my heart your sacred head
your bardo prayers my seat
my silent miles your breath

List of Dreams for Yeshe Walmo

Dead mouthed,
I stain red pillows
with drool.
Tape my lips.
My list of dreams
bore dreams.
They found me, bent
me, broke my face,
turned sons
to grandmothers,
trees to saviors,
daughters
to fathers, fire
to prayers.
Better not to list
one's dreams.
This moment
the required dream.
Shake me, take
my head, bead it
on a twisted cord.
Wear it, blue one,
wake me.

Fish Heads

Ted Fish made heads out of clay.
He was known for it, loved.
These heads are all over Salida.
Pinch lipped busts in shop windows.
Bobbing ornaments in dead trees.
One, a skinless, meat-red monolith
sits on a bank among boulders,
casting the line of its low gaze
over the Arkansas, a marker
for boaters to measure depth.
I never knew him except through
others' grief. He died a few
weeks before I moved there.
On the table. Under the knife.
His heart.

Two heads came into my hands
in round about ways. One
from a new friend, fellow artist
and co-worker, Ben, whose
eyes teared up when he handed
it to me, a porcelain, grimacing,
two-faced thing with a hole
clear through the crown to
the throat, passage for some jute
rope I've planned for years to string
with fat, glass beads the color
of Caribbean swells. Maybe

I'll finally get to it. After a story,
Barbara, poet who refuses
public farewells and left his funeral
early, gave me the other: a black face—
blue edged, sort of grinning—emerging
from white porcelain slab. The whole
thing attached to a small black canvas
with two long copper wire stitches.
I placed it on the piano where sheet
music should perch. The piano
is always out of tune, but my son
plays it anyway. Two nights ago,

on a stop as he was driving through,
the tiny head rang, watery
with my son's invented song.

When I hugged him hello
and later goodbye, hard, I felt him
tremble, quaking in the core, a dark
face pressing through his body
into mine. In the kitchen, he talked
in low, steady tones, like there
was earth under his feet, said
when he gets back he's drying out,
going to stop filling the hole
with every dead sailor in the sea.
"You can do it," I said, "change karma,
consequence." Which was too much,
another hole. *You can do it* is all I meant,
but saying less is hard for me. He knows.
"Thank you," he said, and for a second,
soft eyed, lost himself among crumbs
on the counter. Then raised his head.

after Raymond Carver

Dissolve

Walking the Burn

Here the roots blew,
sent milk quartz flying.

And here quartz fields are untouched,
surrounded by a ring of char.

I want to say my love is quartz with no reason
for what is spared but wind and water.

Everywhere are black skeletons
of juniper, more beautiful stripped and stark.

They'll stand a hundred years.
Nothing will eat them. They don't rot.

I want to say each one
is a word in my hardest love story.

Here, the ancient ponderosa in its black skin and arms,
hope already drilled from its massive trunk.

The flow beneath singed bark bleeds sweet sap.
Though needles on high are green, it won't survive.

I want to say its beetles
are my apologies.

Here is where wild grasses stopped
burning. Step over the amazing line.

What burned a month ago is now
greener than what was saved.

I want to say that field is my face
before and after you.

Mountain Monsoon

Loud seconds turned ten minutes white.
Ice marbles shredded pines, and hundreds,

no, many thousands of tiny piñon cones
dropped like fists across flagstone paths

and bounced in drunken dance with hail
through carefully tended beds. Blood roses,

poppies, lilies, coneflowers, daisies,
hollyhocks, pots of mint, tomato, petunias,

basil, sage—all torn, bruised, deflowered
by odd stones, assault tangled up in rain

and new needles, everything now a sodden,
sad mulch. The quadrennial promise of pine

nuts lost—days later, ragged hands of hostas
raised a stand of pale poles. Purple buds

hung limp above green tatters, never bloomed
in surrender. Fire ants collected their nectar.

Pietà

Smoke is filling up the valley.
The Sangre de Cristo mountains
disappear, erupt from rust
like the ragged rosary in my chest
I am always fingering like Mary
remembering the perfect beads
of Jesus' newborn toes. Ten, ten,
how many times she counted,
kissed, wished to gobble them.
How many times she washed
his hairy feet. She must have been
at least 50. Old, outgrown, holding
the broken man across her lap,
his bony limbs a liquid stiffening
into the form of her final cradle.

Keen

One day our flesh and bone were nearly,
then dearly, cut away by hands we made.

One day strange hands filleted our breasts,
beloved friends, from our narrow rib cage.

Our men hold ground, grasp our feet
lifting off, pull us down from pain to arms,

from frayed rope, from blood, from knife,
from gun smoke, from sky, from fruitless hope.

Sisters! we cry, mountains away, our hands
too far to reach each other's face and crown.

Distance requires wailing into phones
No no, no no, breath-broke, broken stones

rolling through our animal throats—pitched
grief washed voices only women know.

Do not mistake this duet for a song. If flesh
were not going or already gone, if someone

stood outside our panes of glass, peered in,
watched the scene unfold in silent mime:

our hands pressing slim machines
against our ears, our pacing out a pattern

on the rug, our gaping mouths, spasm spines,
eyes clamped shut, heads thrown back

could be mistaken for our ancient belly laugh.

You Can Fill a Jar to the Top Twice

1.

Here, among the living, I speak to the mothers
of the dead. Seek out bouquets of hairy nettle,

contemplate the healing sting. Pinch off leaves
with thumb and pointer finger, gently, gently,

unstung. Or, in your rush, learn the joy of green
burn, that dull lingering. Spread this medicine

on a tray. Dry your gatherings in the dark.
By crackling fistful, drop them in a quart jar,

top them off with boiling water. Lid the brew.
Steep four hours. Drink deep to reach the ache

in your sobbing, perimenopausal womb
where the child once swam and breathed you.

2.

Here among the living, I speak to the mothers
of the dead. Valerian rises under the plum tree.

You didn't expect a scent so sweet, white blooms!
You had to look it up, learn what to do: uproot

the long primeval stalks, smell the roots, wash
them in your kitchen sink and chop until the whole

house smells of teenage boy socks: colossal,
sacred, reeking feet. Grab a wide mouth Mason.

Pack it to the brim with roots. Fill it full, again,
with your favorite spirit: vodka, brandy, rum. Steep

six weeks. Sleepless, spoon it stinging, stinking,
under your tongue. Hold it there, burn. Lie down.

Circle the umbel of sleep. Press your cheek
against the soft in-between, lost queen. Nestle in.

Dream him

for Rosemerry

Blue Daughters

There are blue daughters
        my daughter cannot save.
Hanging from hand knit scarf
        and pink bunk bed,
Found by a little sister
        after Pokemon and macaroni;
Or carried in on Saturday
        by a running father
Damning Monday when
        his daughter's flu turns
Hot pneumonia,
        limping sepsis. Pulseless.

Fast, I see her humming
        over small bodies,
Measuring every nuance:
        pupil, grimace, shade
Of skin, curl of leg.
        At once a warm machine
Pumping, hands I have held
        become small hearts.
Her voice hopeful, urging
        sweeties, honeys, kiddos
To breathe, open eyes,
        cry in confusion
At the sterile room,
        the crowded bedroom
Full of stuffed bears,
        Barbies, strangers,
Parents in the corner
        of the nightmare.

When thirty minutes pass,
        drops form
On her upper lip,
        inside her dark blue shirt.
She cycles in and out
        with her best friends
Who've learned
        to massage death in turns,

With cheers and sighs
        for fragile victories,
Knowing eyes for the dark
        unmooring dawning.

Hours of engine hands
        and pulsing drugs,
Electric volts of science,
        love,
And existential prayer
        may be not enough.
Personnel wipe
        their lowered faces, pause;
Stiffly leave the room
        where plastic tubes,
Blood-stained gauze,
        tiny clothes litter the floor.

My daughter, ever tidy as a girl,
        knows the simple
Magic of mundane order:
        cleans the mess,
Lifts the child from floor
        to lower bunk, arranges
Silken hair around a bruised neck,
        brushes wisps
From the blue girl's
        precious forehead.
When the crush-faced mother
        crawls in bed
With her still daughter,
        my daughter goes, must
Go. Tall. Departs the room,
        the house, the hospital.
Calls me, bright voice cracking,
        on the drive home.

47

To the touch, my face feels
like a bloated marshmallow
when I wake, the kind
about to slip its skin over fire.
Puffy, warm, loose. Not so
fine lines and nearsightedness
combine to make memories rise.
My mother's voice in her late 40s,
50s, 60s, 70s, before her vanity
on a small red-cushioned
wrought iron stool
in the master bathroom,
magnifying mirror parked
like a giant goblet of mercury.
Hearing my morning approach,
lifting a folded, cold wash cloth
off her eyes, wide blue and bright
with disgust at her body's betrayal,
she would bark, "Look at these eyes!"
and jab an accusing finger
at her soft face, not the mirror,
that has always loved me.

The Night Before I Turned 51

I dreamed my father next to me
holding my hand through a parking lot,
his full cheeked smile held inside
those radiating parentheses reaching
out like endless arms from his eyes—
like mine in the brightest sunlight,
caught laughing in a rearview mirror.
(I learned to love my smile by loving his.)
We walked like this toward some store
I wanted to avoid, so he wouldn't feel
he had to buy me something, the coat
I wanted, or some other ephemeral
thready thing to make up for a lifetime
of missing him, missing him, missing him.
I rehearsed in my mind what I wanted
him to know: *I forgive you every day.*
I woke before I said it, distracted by
a gallery of Japanese woodcut prints,
one of them a curious face watching us
pass as I noticed us drift across glass.

Hagstone

On the beach we all have a knack for something.
My son in law skips stones six leaps across a thinning surf.
My husband harbors inner heat despite the wind.
With ease I find black stones with holes clear through
where witches live, my daughter says, and laughs.
Her gifted ears are fine tuned to tumbling staffs
of waves crashing in multi-phonic whispers and roars.
Harmonics hum along this stretch of sand, lost on me.
My ever gulping pupils ignore my poor ears, grow
lost in mirages of hands and feet burning in the campfire,
wood mimicking bone, an archeology of grain
that striates everything, as though the whole earth
were breathing inside a set of giant, fractal ribs
spinning out the endless chests of gulls, men, fish,
metastasized hotels, pretty cages glowing along
the coast like mammoth corpses or gum-receded teeth.
Red logs remind me how many degrees my bones
will reach on the path to ash, ash my family may choose
to suspend in blown glass, spun globes to place on desks
as paperweights, or shelves as funerary art or shrines
beneath thangkas of Tapihritsa where I may serve
as a reminder, a gutted clock. Perched on a mirror base,
plugged in, LED lit, five alternating colored lights
shining through what's left of me, a tiny spiral galaxy,
starry crumbs of my body glowing in vitreous space
like Tibetan thigles, to everyone's surprise I will be
not quite a comfort, not quite discomfiting.

The Last Cut in Our Limited Series

A shared glance of joie de vivre
then turning back to what we do:
the book, the broom, the pen, the seed,
the plate, the drill, the trail, the moon,
the sprout, the dog, the tune, the leaf,
the pill, the wash, the snow, the croon,
the call, the pan, the sigh, the cream,
the tea, the cloud, the deer, the room,
the egg, the wine, the bill, the screen,
the sink, the child, the road, the bloom,
the grill, the pine, the hen, the weed,
the wood, the soil, the hand, the shoe,
the fire, the nap, the cat, the creek,
the bowl, the knife, the rib, the coop,
the prayer, the salt, the dome, the peak,
the leg, the rhyme, the fish, the tooth,
the smoke, the time, the rain, the sleep,
adieu, adieu, adieu, adieu.

for Dorell

Kids and Dogs

When you have kids and dogs,
that's all you have, a grandmother told
her daughter once, who later told me,
a young mother bemoaning the slow
disintegration of my precious things.
Dog-scratched leather couch.
Ripped loveseat. Urine scented rugs.
Walls smeared with strawberry jam.
Shattered handmade ceramic bowls.
Vomit-stained, dog-haired car upholstery.
Kitchen table scarred by knives and forks.
I fantasized a future in which my stuff
survived mayhem. Now it has arrived.
I can guarantee: when you have kids
and dogs, you don't even have them.

Rebeccanrachel

From time to time someone will learn my name
at a conference or wedding, shake my hand,
and later, in passing, call me that other famous
Old Testament name, warmly embedded
in a sentence: *Rebecca, how long have you taught art?*
or, *What is your connection to the bride, Rebecca?*
I'll smile, say, *It's Rachel, but it's ok*, and they'll apologize
until I explain I love to be called my little sister's name
and often was, as a girl, by work weary parents,
sounding off the litany of four to seven children's names
depending on which home we were visiting
or living in, until the right one landed on the ears
of the wayward, beloved one. *Yes,* I say, *it's ok
to call me by her name.* I love to hear the song
of it in the air, to remember the years when we were
Rachelnrebecca, to wear it for her, hear it in the flesh
we share as sisters, as if being composed
of mostly the same stuff were enough to live her,
give her an aging body, hard-won love,
the joy and grief of bearing, raising, sparing children
our inheritance, as if by surrogacy, by baptismal proxy,
rising every morning from the water of my bed.

Holding On

Can you tell a green field
From a cold steel rail?
Do you think you can tell?
~Roger Waters

in my early 30s I found a letter
in my dead sister's boxes
my father had written
during her honduran mission:
"rachel is lost," he'd said.
i still I wonder at his—at her—
smug surety of a way, holding on
to the rod, the iron rod of mormon lore
i sculpted once in early college—
a frieze in low relief, rod receding
in one point perspective, skirting
a great and spacious building—
the rod that rhymes with god in hymns,
not the psalmist's bludgeon
shattering sinners like pottery,
but lehi's dream of a handrail,
the one i hoped would keep me
on a righteous path, headed
for a flaming tree. i let it go,
that cold rail, it's true, that story
i lived in for a time, that borrowing
we told ourselves. i let go the rod
for broad sky, like my son,
now driving toward oregon,
feeling lost, he told his father,
trying to figure it out, without knowing
what he's trying to figure out,
which makes me think he has arrived
like i once did, not lost, dear fathers,
but alive, knee aching, armpits
stinking of onions, tapestries filtering
morning light through rolled up windows,
preparing to bathe by spray bottle
in a walmart parking lot, that bardo
where no one lingers long,
holding on to a wheel.

for Grey

Crossing Tacoma Bridges
with My Pregnant Daughter

I notice moss in the cracks of the peeling white footbridge.
Its wooden arms reach across the tracks of trains
that crawl through the belly of Titlow Park. We stop,
hands on the railing, look down, look into the woods
where tracks disappear, look through foliage to the Sound.
Days later, on another walk over Narrows Bridge, I notice twin
crisscross symmetries of early metal towers perched on piers
mirroring newer concrete ones; sage green suspension cables—
sloped, parallel, curving pipes she says her family of firefighters
climb, clipped into handrails, to the tops of tower saddles
where they rappel to the Sound to practice emergency
rescue. It is my privilege to notice only moss and eras
of architecture after a bridge has collapsed, to feel my nerves
jolt with the thought of her precarious ascents and descents.

Beneath, or perhaps, transparently overlaid like thin skin
upon these rare moments of our togetherness, my daughter
also sees bodies leapt upon tracks, a beloved, sad dispatcher
scattered by a train, crushed women and men floating
on the Sound that rushed up like pure despair, that liquid body
like unforgiving, then forgiving, concrete. Every so many yards,
a sign is posted on the bridge that makes a promise:
"There is always hope," followed by a number to call
that ends with TALK. We don't. Standing there, suspended,
we span memories of a bullet hole in a wooden floor,
a hoodie pulled up to spare our eyes a rope burned neck.
We take in the view of the ragged, verdant shore, our ears
lashed by traffic's knives. She says, "I can still hear the frogs….
Listen, what is that called?" Susurrus, I say. We pause. Listen.

Sand Burial

Before tractors buried my father
who would have loved to watch the work
of those machines, earthmovers, like himself—
the way good men pulled levers to lift his vault lid,
suspended like a Frank Lloyd Wright cantilever
hovering over the eternal balcony of death,
that bardo where inside marries outside,
and lowered one end perfectly above him
until one lip slipped into the vault's rim
and made the opposite end quaver
(*That's how you know male meets female*,
the undertaker said with pride in his men,
artists, he called them, for knowing
the subtle arts of the trade: *See, that's when
they know the concrete seam will seal, their signal
to lower the lid the rest of the way*)—
I stood with Sam in his grandpa's Quicksilver cap,
grey hairs and spiced sweat still in the band,
threw fistfuls of Utah sand into the hole
then shovelfuls, to finally let his chronic absence go,
resurrecting now the memory of that day my father
fished small grains of Illinois sand from my red eyes
with tissue he had wadded to a point,
that tenderness, the lingering sting.

Eclipse '24, for Grey, 24

He has sought
the path of totality,
my son.

He has built
an infrastructure
to worship it,

laid down ropes of power
for the festival.
He will stand beneath

the darkened sun
whole.
He knows now,

it doesn't last long.
I know now,
he will come home.

A raven will shout
something dark
about awe.

Confluence

The river enters my son
becomes his hair, runs long
behind his ears, over shoulders

enters his sweat, wet raft scent of hugs
lingers on my face and arms
drifts in rooms when he departs

becomes the wisdom of his limbs
his thoughts a paddle turned a fraction
slim-edged deflection of a current that can kill

broad blade, he tunes himself against it
leans into it, slides past deep shadows
sucking underneath giant boulders

hones each edge of his heart, river muscle
a living rudder, minutely responsive
the boat only a boat but more

his joy, that brave buoyance
carries us past ancient reversals, smokers
sleepers, undercuts, widow makers

that stoic face water-cut in canyon wall
a story, a foil to his countenance
eyes sparkling, scouting the line

for Sam

Four Days Past Due

Rhododendrons burst baby pink,
lavender, fuchsia and maroon. Roses too.
Even beet-red peonies snipped short
to fit the fat jar—five cervixes on green stems—
open within hours of being arranged—
like spring—on cue. But the body is not
a simple flower turning to light. A child
is not a scent or fruit. He turns inside his mother,
not the mysterious worm in a jumping bean,
not the wet butterfly finishing his wings,
not the eye inside a closed lid, dreaming
while the muffled world calls and sings
his name to wake, hatch, bloom. He knows
no metaphors, this water being. His mother
is no tree, bush, jar, socket, pod, but a woman
surrounded by flowers, warm inside, abiding,
living in her own time, smiling silently
at the advice of mothers young and old:
try sex, mountain hikes, spicy burritos,
clary sage, birth ball bouncing, castor oil,
masturbation, nipple stimulation,
stairs, curb walks, this acupressure point.
She carries on quietly, amused, not the spring
her mother imagines, not the moon on two legs,
but a woman weeding her real garden
of invasive green, pulling ferns, English ivy,
wild raspberries beneath apple trees,
her strong thighs parted, straddling a giant belly.
Scratched, resting, cooled, she spoons
peanut butter onto boats of medjool dates,
savors, swallows, softens in her own way,
embracing, with me, the first and last lesson
of motherhood: be present while you wait.

Mother Dharma

A child is a slow
moving thought
you watch.

Its departing birth
a new entrance,
inching back
into into into you.

You surrender
your eyes, let it
commandeer hands,
arms and legs,
eat your heart,
guts and brain,
become your bones,
your size, watch it
dissolve into a dazzling
dangerous world,
into its own child.

Helpless, welcome
it like sky burial:
child into child
into child burial.

Embrace the lineage
of generous forgetting,
your liberation.

Dissolving the Body

Brown curls fade like meteors
Across an inner sky.
My head, a solid thought of starlings,
Parts and spreads.
Fingers fizzle out like sparklers in July.
Arms swirl like sand bars
Stolen by midnight prairie flood.
There goes my heart, a shattered
Glass in slow motion rainbow.
Blood, what becomes of blood? Mist?
Lungs disperse like a careless cough.
My lunch is carried off in my guts
By invisible vultures.
Hips loosen their grip on motherhood's
Lingering ache and break into light.
My legs explode and lift
Like two burst pillows in a gust of wind.
These feet go walking as dust into dust
In a million glinting rays.
My stories move and move through
Edgeless space like radio waves
Transmitting all the tongues and songs
And breaking news and silly sitcoms
Of humankind. I laugh a laughless
Laugh track, completely uncanned.

Notes

p. 39: "Kate Chopin's Women" is a reference to characters who broke free of patriarchal Victorian culture: Edna of *The Awakening*, first published in 1899, and Calixta, in the steamy short story "The Storm," composed in 1898 but not published in Chopin's lifetime. It first appeared in print in 1969. My personal cherished collection of these works is *The Awakening and Selected Stories*, Penguin Books, 1984.

p. 47: The title "Who am I Now that I have Forgiven You?" comes from the final line in Sharon Old's poem "After 37 Years My Mother Apologizes for My Childhood," in *The Gold Cell*, Alfred A. Knopf, 1990.

p. 48: "To My Mother" by Wendell Berry, from *Entries*, Pantheon Books, 1994.

p. 59: The multiple-choice format is inspired by A.E. Stallings's "First Love: A Quiz," from HAPAX: POEMS, Evanston: TriQuarterly Books/Northwestern University Press, 2006.

p. 64: *A rural, local football team is called the Beetdiggers. Fans refer to themselves as "Diggers."

I wrote this poem as an example of pastiche for my American Literature students. The goal of this end-of-semester assignment was to link our own poetic voice and experience to that of other American writers. All excerpts in this poem are from *The Heath Anthology of American Literature*, Concise, 1st Edition, edited by Paul Lauter.

p. 68: Trudier Harris's essay "The Trickster in African American Literature" is published on the National Humanities Center website: www.nationalhumanitiescenter.org/tserve/freedom/1865-1917/essays/trickster.htm

p. 77: Excerpted from the entry for Eastern Towhee in the *National Geographic Field Guide to the Birds of North America*, 3rd edition.

p. 88: Dick Lourie's poem "forgiving our fathers," from *Ghost Radio*, Hanging Loose Press, 1998. I first became familiar with an adapted excerpt of it in the final scene of *Smoke Signals*, a film directed by Chris Eyre from a screenplay by Sherman Alexie. I watch it every year. I cry every time.

p. 91: The epigraph is an excerpt from Chris Whitley's song, "Dust Radio," from the album *Living with the Law*, Columbia Records, 1991.

p. 93: Galway Kinnell's poem "Saint Francis and the Sow," from *Three Books*, Houghton Mifflin Company, 2002.

p. 94: The references to Virginia Woolf's characters, Clarissa and Septimus, come from her 1925 novel *Mrs. Dalloway*, and the gendernaut, Orlando, from her 1928 novel of the same name. My beloved copies of these books were printed in 1976 and 1977, respectively, by Grafton Books.

p. 101: *Adrienne Rich, from "The Blue Ghazals," in *The Will to Change*, 1971.

p. 103: The song I allude to in this poem, "River," by Leon Bridges, is from his album *Coming Home*, Columbia Records, 2015. The referenced video, gorgeously and cinematically produced by Smuggler OPC, can be viewed at: www.youtube.com/watch?v=0Hegd4xNfRo&t=7s

p. 106: Yeshe Walmo is a female protector deity of the Yungdrung Bön Buddhist tradition, of which I have been a practitioner for nearly twenty years.

p. 108: I love Raymond Carver's clipped phrases and no-nonsense storytelling through poetry and thought I'd give it a try.

p. 121: Tapihritsa (c 7th-8th century) is an enlightened master of the Bön tradition, believed to have attained rainbow body upon his death, and thigles are luminous, rainbow spheres that spontaneously appear in one's natural mind while engaged in the Dzogchen practice of tögal.

p. 125: "Wish You Were Here," lyrics by Roger Waters, from the album *Wish You Were Here*, Harvest Records, 1975.

Acknowledgements

2025
"Walking the Burn" in Twenty Bellows' spring anthology, *We Are the West: Embers*

2022
"Reteach a Thing Its Loveliness," "Little Rachel Dreams of Regeneration," "The Old Phones," "Family Organism," "List of Dreams for Yeshe Walmo," "Mother Dharma," "D-Con," in *Mad Blood* #7, a literary and visual arts collection published by Thornlyre Arts

2015
"Tiny Birds," third place winner of the Margo Award in the National Federation of State Poetry Societies Contest, in the 2015 NFSPS anthology, *Encore*

2008
"Because my son announces Narnia trees! on his seventh winter solstice," *A Prairie Journal* (Winter)

"To My Little Sister, Dying," *Barnwood International Poetry Magazine*

Special Thanks

During the years my sons struggled with severe mental health crises, writing was a safe haven, a place to process that harrowing experience. Thankfully, they have developed skills to navigate their neurodiversity and nurture stability, but I've felt very hesitant to share the poems that emerged in that time. As I tentatively curated this manuscript, however, threads and patterns emerged, unveiling difficult issues that run deep in our family history, much larger than any one of us. Buoyed by this realization, I sought my sons' insight on how to proceed. They both lovingly encouraged me to include poems about their challenges, explaining that suicide is the epidemic of their generation. Our hope is that by being transparent about our family's experience, others will benefit and share in our fragile tenacity. Thank you, Grey and Sam, for your trust and permission to share our story, for your inspiring courage to rise from the fire and forge authentic, rich lives.

Thank you, Dorell, for your unwavering love, warmth, and support. Thank you, Sage, for your wisdom, strength and friendship. Thank you, George, for being a loving father and friend through it all. Thank you, Shane and Indigo, my bonus daughters, for your moxie, for loving us across the miles. Thank you, Carson and Cal, for the joy you bring. Thank you, Kimmi, for your humor, honesty and sisterhood. Thank you, Becca, for the gift of your life, the teachings of your death. Thank you to my mother for your unconditional love and faith, to my father whose absence shaped me like a vase, and to my stepfather, Lahne, for being there. To all my relatives and ancestors, thank you for your part in our family's fractal dance: may we all heal in the spirit of *amor fati* and *becoming*. And thank you, dear friends and teachers, especially Tenzin Wangyal Rinpoche, who stand by us, call out the best in us.

Where would I be without my Colorado poetry family? I am so grateful for the decades we've shared, keeping the poetry fire burning across the state. Thank you, Barbara Ford, for your writing companionship. Thank you, Peter Anderson and Everett Wilson, for your notes on early drafts of this book. Thank you, Julie Cummings, for your keen eye. Thank you, Rosemerry Wahtola Trommer, for welcoming me to this poetry family, for gently midwifing and introducing this collection to the world. You are an astounding light. And finally, thank you, David Martin of Middle Creek Publishing, for taking my fledgling book under your wing and patiently giving it flight.

To space, our mother, who holds and pervades us all: thank you for every word.

About the Author

Rachel Kellum lives with her family at the foot of the Sangre de Cristo mountains where she has made a life teaching greenhouse gardening, visual and language arts to valley children, writing at Adams State University, and humanities and literature courses for Trinidad State College. For seven years running, she and a posse of local poets have put on the Crestone Poetry Festival. Kellum earned a BFA in Art from Millikin University and an MA in English from Colorado State. Her career began as an English and art instructor at Morgan Community College for eleven years, during which time she served six years as director of the MCC CACE Gallery of Fine Art and host of Open Mic Poetry Nights, featuring Colorado's finest poets. A Pushcart Prize nominee and NFSPS award winning poet, her poetry has been featured in several online journals and print collections. She leads writing workshops, performs her poetry around Colorado and blogs at wordweeds.com. Her first book, *ah*, published by Liquid Light Press, was released in 2012.

About the Press

Middle Creek Publishing believes that responding to the world through art & literature—and sharing that response—is a vital part of being an artist.

Middle Creek Publishing is a company seeking to make the world a better place through both the means and ends of publishing. We are publishers of quality literature in any genre from authors and artists, both seasoned and those who are undiscovered or under-valued, or under-represented, with a great interest in works which illuminate or embody any aspect of contemplative Human Ecology, defined as the relationship between humans and their natural, social, and built environments.

Middle Creek Publishing's particular interest in Human Ecology is meant to clarify an aspect of the quality in the works we will consider for publication and as a guide to those considering submitting work to us. Our interest is in publishing works which illuminate the human experience through words, story or other content that connects us to each other, our environment, our history, and our potential deeply and more consciously.

www.ingramcontent.com/pod-product-compliance
Lightning Source LLC
Chambersburg PA
CBHW080604170426
43196CB00017B/2897